LWG POETRY ANTHOLOGY
2024

By Members of Letchworth Writers Group

The parent organisation of Letchworth Writers Group is the Letchworth Arts and Leisure Group (LALG). Writers have been meeting for many years. Prior to the Pandemic in 2020 members met in person, latterly in Mrs Howard Memorial Hall in Norton Way South. During the Pandemic in 2020, meetings moved online, and they have remained online via Zoom ever since. The majority of members find online meetings more convenient, and it also means that those who have moved away from the Letchworth area can continue to attend.

Letchworth Writers meet on the first Tuesday evening each month. In advance of the meeting members submit a piece of writing – prose, short story, section of a novel, memoir, non-fiction, poetry, play. At the meeting, members introduce their work and read all or part. Other members will then comment and discuss in a supportive way.

Poetry in this Anthology represents work written by members between 2021 and 2024.

If anyone would like to join Letchworth Writers Group please contact letchworthwritersonline@gmail.com

Published in 2024 by Letchworth Writers Group

Compiled by Paul Walker

ISBN: 9798328647892

TABLE OF CONTENTS

Dedication to Len Maynard
1953 – 2023
By Davina Frame

Len joined the Letchworth Writers Group in 2018 and jointly facilitated the meetings with Paul Walker. He set up and managed the group website, compiled anthologies and published and supported the group's work.

Born in Enfield, north London, in 1953, Len Maynard wrote and published over 50 books. He started writing when he was 20, teaming up with school friend Mick Sims. They started out writing short stories together as Maynard Sims and formed a small publishing house, Enigmatic Press. They edited two series of horror story magazines, attended lots of conventions and were interviewed by magazines and radio shows. They went on to write over 40 novels together: ghost story collections; the Department 18 series of supernatural thrillers; stand-alone horror novels; the Bahamas series of action-adventure thrillers; and a handful of standalone thrillers. As editors, they were responsible for the *Enigmatic Tales* and *Darkness Rising* series of anthologies, as well as single anthologies in the horror and crime genres. The six *DCI Jack Callum* mysteries, set in London and Hertfordshire during the 1950's and 1960's, were the first to be written under Len's own name.

When Mick decided to scale back his writing and publishing activities, Len decided it was time to branch out under his own name and LMP - Len Maynard Publishing was born. Initially conceived as a vehicle to publish his own work, it wasn't long before the desire to publish the very talented authors he had become aquainted with over the years became too strong to resist. From children's books through to crime, adventures and sci-fi he threw open the doors to encourage, support and publish their work. A touching memory for me was his compilation of memories and photos from a man I knew through the

9

Letchworth Hospice. Len published *Sid's Wonderful Life;* a gift of generosity that made an old man very happy.

Len was my best friend for 25 years. A cuddly, teddy bear of a man whose invitations to, "fancy dinner and a few classics on my big TV?" were always welcome. Len's humour could have me in fits of laughter, his insight and generosity of spirit was remarkable. But more than all that… boy could he tell a story!

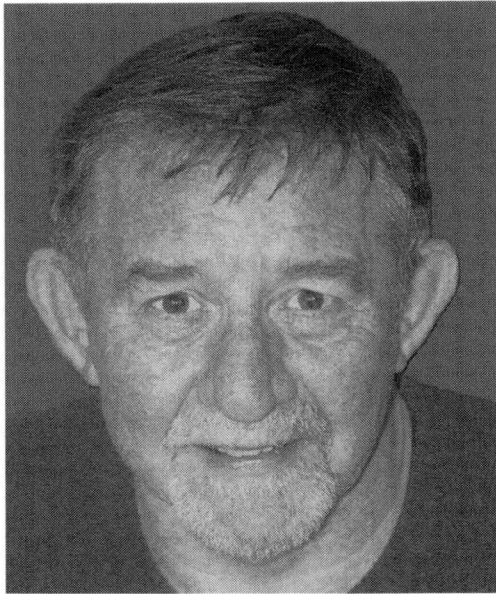

Remembrance

By Davina Frame

My heart hurts.
Often silent, calm and at rest
unexpectedly it turns cold like a stone in my chest.
News of similar sadness should create turmoil and sorrow
but there is no pattern or prediction of what may follow.
It's often the remembrance of a meeting, a fun-filled exchange
that brings forth the most tears and mental pain.
Why do the things that should make me smile
crush and break me again and again?

Love lost is better than none had to lose
is the so-called wisdom of those that choose
to pine for lovers that left them alone
seeking comfort that they too were loved once and so
they remember the joy and adoration
the attention and expectation
a badge worn to soothe the feelings low.
Their lost loves live on and in time they will too
replacing the loved one with someone quite new.

But for us, who mourn the loss and feel the pain
of all those ripped from our lives so suddenly it's plain
that no comfort from death of such kind can be gained.
The finality of their absence can't be explained or exchanged.
Instead, we hope that someday time will heal and ease
our broken hearts and show us how to smile again in peace.

I will always love you and miss you so much.
My little sister, my best friend, the loves I loved, my crutch
I'll never forget your being or stop longing for your touch.
To have known you and held you in my heart for so many years
was the blessing you gave me then and worth all these tears.

In remembrance of my sister Karen 19/7/23 and best friend Len 11/11/23

A Day in Her Life
By Stephen Turner

Through a gap, in the curtain, there came the sun's early morning ray,
She stirred, still abed, half-asleep, wondering, who shall I marry today?
And, after a moment, she scratched and arose, stretching the night away,
And saw, in the mirror, her slip askew, bleary eyes, her hair with whisps
　　of grey,
Her small breasts accentuated by silk: can they be sagging yet, for she
　　thought that they may.
Staggered to the bathroom, gathered up last night's keks - thrown down
　　– where they lay.
Ensconced on the throne – a damn cold throne! - she wondered again:
　　who shall I marry today?

Yoghurt, granola, fresh-squeezed fruit; what shall I eat?
Looking across a table of last evening's mess, and seeing that ever-
　　empty seat,
What would they think of this for a life, every morning, the person I
　　meet?
Looking across this table at me! Scruffy. Smelly? Dish-washered hands
　　and naked, tight-shoed feet,
Could anyone cherish me – for forty years – and still see me as a long
　　life's treat!
My grey hair, my rough hands, my bad habits, my marmaladed face –
　　unmade – blank as the sheet,
Who, I wonder, should ever wish to occupy – to gaze on me from - that
　　opposite empty seat?

Down, past the Archway, down the Holloway Road, still half-trapped in
　　the night,

Carrying her document case. Shall I be noticed today, be promoted? Is it true that I might?

Up in the lift, to the twentieth floor. Into the office; to the screen flickering with half-intelligent light,

Did anyone speak, say "hallo", say anything – human to human – no matter how little or slight?

Did her boss ever say: "Well Done!", "You did Great!" "We much appreciate your getting that right!"

Did they say "We're promoting you today. There's a pay rise too, though the competition was tight".

Only in this way did she survive, dreaming the morning away. Could it really be true that they might!

They gathered for lunch, in a dark bar; she, lodged in a dark corner; down Caledonian Road,

She had applied some lipstick, some rouge, that morning; though in the gloom none of it showed,

She nodded, and smiled - hoped it would do - as the hubbub passed by her - ebbed as it flowed,

Unregarded, unconsulted, unconsidered, unnoticed, uneverything! So little she glowed,

Nibbling a sandwich, the occasional crisp, sipping a drink, existing in a contrived sociable mode,

Wondering about the afternoon: whether promotion would lead to a fret-laden, stress-laden load.

Yet, as life in general, if she had any qualities of beauty, of excellence, perhaps none of it showed.

Tired. It was dark, when she mounted the stairs, struggled in her bag, at last found the key,

Entered her cold apartment. Closed out the world. Wondered, yes, really, who might marry me!

Cast off her shoes. Damn, what a relief! Ate just a little. Dozed just a little. Turned on, to see,

What might be on tele. Checked on her e-mails. Showered. Read a little,
    but only fitfully,
Stripped off for bed, saw herself, again, in the mirror, wondered: hell,
    who am I going to be?
Looked, sideways on, at her figure, at her nakedness, wondered once
    more who could agree
That she was beautiful. That she had anything to give. Asked again, who
    will marry me?

Yet, the poet, writing this, does faithfully believe
She was more beautiful, more lovely, more life-enhancing, this
    daughter of Eve,
And this: what she dreams of, she can entirely achieve.
For, of love, she <u>*can*</u> *give, and truly, of love, she can most certainly*
    receive.

Richard

By Diana Newson

The first time I saw Richard I was en route.
He said,
What happened last night, I can't remember anything at all.
I said,
Nothing happened Richard, and you said nothing at all.
The afternoon passed like a dream,
and I thought, Why am I here? I could be at home, alone.
And he thought the same thing.

The next time I saw Richard I had foundered.
We said,
It's good to see you again. We can't remember anything at all.
But I
danced with him all night, and I think of him in idle moments.
I wonder, what do you want Richard?
and I love your mouth, I love your mouth, I love your mouth,
and come for me, come for me, come for me.

The Wilding

By Paul Green

Letchworth grows wild
the Garden devours the City
as three mighty magnets
entombed by cunning Ebenezer
(to intersect at Ley level
under the Avenue's sprouting brickwork)
create green-lit anomalies
now children feed the brontosaurs
grazing on Norton Common
a fox with a floral hat
patrols the Industrial Zone
and maidens in sensible Spirella corsets
waltz slowly down Eastcheap
towards the ruins of Lenin's statue

To My Mother on Her 79th Birthday

By Meher Pocha

As a child I was full of fears
Of dogs and the dark, the unknown
Easily teased into tears
I'd withdraw to worry alone

But you held my hand and walked with me
Reciting poems beside the sea
And showed me I could learn to free
Myself from all self-doubt and dread
To overcome them and instead
Walk tall with firm and easy tread

You taught me to love truth and beauty
To dance, to laugh, to dream
But, ever mindful of my duty,
To help those drowning in life's stream

I've lacked the courage to stand alone
I might even have become a clone
Of the in-crowd, had you not shown
Me how to stand and fight
For what is clearly just and right
Resting only with success in sight

Don't be dazzled by wealth or birth,
You said, they may be empty show
Learn to judge a person's worth
By what they say and do and know

Don't get married unless you are sure
That life with someone will be more
Lovely, you said, than it was before
In this and many another way
The things you used to do and say
Have made me what I am today

Happiness came with my choices
Guided by your many voices
But unlike you, behind the times,
I still write poetry that rhymes

List

By Stephen Turner

Nina

A list:
And, dear Nina, you are the first
For, under the sticky-bob tree we kissed
And I was only five, and just
A child; and though other pig-tails I may have tugged,
I never tugged yours
For we walked, and talked, and may have hugged
And in the bluebell woods we innocently thought
That life, long and idyllic, was all we sought.

May

But puberty found me, as I grew,
So at a barn dance we two were met,
Whence your young breasts I fleetingly knew,
But "top half only" let's not forget!
And like that film – the way we were!
Our paths had crossed, and – as all others - then diverged:
My May! – a fantasy I had of her
That into a harsh reality emerged:
This: first love bears a heavy cost,
For first love is best, but sharpest lost.

B.

My diary names you just as "B",
And of you, B, I this recall,

Our long, long walks – both you and me,
We spoke of all things, good and ill,
And solved life's problems, every one,
Yet never did I hold your hand,
Nor kissed your lips, that never done,
It was mind-to-mind, you understand,
Platonic was the love we knew,
Of physical contact was there none?
Can such a "love" be passionately true?

Janine

And so to Janine,
Who – a young but neurotic friend:
Of her, in '69 I wrote,
Sadly of my love, and – more sadly - of her end.
"She slipped away,
Janine, of the fair, fair face,
And the long, happy summer's day
We knew;
She was borne by the stream
Her long, brown hair diffuse like a dream,
Her lily hands bobbing
On the water's willowed sobbing;
Now the laughter she knew
Was a tiny current murmuring
In the water's brew.

By leafy lanes she paused,
Catching the sun's brief light
On her slight-part lips,
Her hair was caught by the passing flow,
As she in life: wondering which way to go,
Slowly, slowly she turned

In a pool's dead grip;
Now what new secrets
Had she learned?

Janine, won't you speak to me;
Will your smiling eyes
The spires and villages see?
Will a tentative frown
Cross your cheeks
As you pass under bridges
And pause in stagnant creeks?

I regret so much
The passing of fair summer's days;
Janine is a sign
Stirring languidly, her arms, like rays
Spread, toes dipping,
Head turning side to side
As the stream's cross currents ride,
And there, behind,
A slight, slight wake
Of bubbles rising;
Where are you now?
On what brief beach
Have you latched – I know not;
Yet on your fair white brow
The sun's rays call
And on deaf ears fall."

Anonymous: My Purple Woman

She, nameless, came to me in a later time,
        And from a poster there arose this rhyme,
[Written September '79.]

"In what dimension
Shall I measure the purple woman?
In the two I first saw her
Advertised
On the Piccadilly escalator?
There were no takers save I.
Then: gone by.

Months later –
Coming off the 9.22
At Finsbury Park she was there!
Rather smaller than I had thought
Nevertheless the purple woman I had sought,
Sling-back heels, black narrow skirt,
Her eyes caught mine
Waiting at the Moorgate line.

Purple woman, red skies,
Brown nights and her green green eyes
In ever surprise,
Truth from love's mauve lies
Made us dawn-orange wise.

Length breadth height,
Purple woman,
She is gone from me – late –
But sometimes I see her
Distantly, not quite as before,
The purple woman haunts me it seems,
In what dimension shall I measure my dreams?"

Stephanie

And so to my old age, and to the end:

Stephanie,
Who was my bride, my mistress, my confidante, my greatest friend,
Whereas the others are fantasies,
Of this I tell, and truly feel,
You were my one and greatest love,
And thankfully so completely real.

[Author's note: the "film" referred to in the second verse, "May", is that wonderfully powerful piece of creative writing, music, and performing: "Brassed Off" (1996, Mark Herman) in which the young lovers are so well played by Ewan McGregor and Tara Fitzgerald.]

Inner sound

By Diana Newson

Twelve years old
        in the summer garden
I announced:
"Silence has a sound".

No one else
        heard those Aeolian harps.
At twenty-five
I knew its name.

Tinnitus.

Many Ingredients
By Erol Hasan

We need people who are comfortable with bodily parts and functions,
To heal, and to care for, the sick and disabled;
Also, those with a strong concern for morality,
To judge right from wrong, and to administer justice;
Strong, streetwise, individuals with a cool nerve,
To patrol the streets, and to protect the public;
Risktakers, and creative thinkers,
To achieve, and to inspire, advancement and success;
People-watchers, to recognise the mental health issues
That affect not only individuals, but society as a whole;
Circumspect thinkers, to put life into perspective,
And to identify opportunities and hazards;
Artists, to express the beauty of life,
To engage our imagination,
And to nourish our souls;
And practical types, to make and maintain the entities
That facilitate safe and effective day-to-day functioning…
And many others.

How terrible it is, when an ease with the inner body
Is directed with malice,
To harm, rather than to heal;
Or when those who judge are cruel and lack humility,
Punishing excessively, or perverting the spirit of faith;
Or, when those charged to keep us safe,
Abuse their power and status;
When teachers bully, or repress,
The very people who have come to trust their word and example!

Should we question the fabric of our own, and collective, being?
Sometimes, things go wrong;
Danger is part of life's tapestry,
And a consequence of the random way in which
Personal characteristics, and events, combine and mutate;
It is one of the most powerful motivating forces we have;
We live with the possibility of misfortune and damage,
However undeserved and grotesque the experience can be;
A flourishing, and responsible, human race
Requires many diverse ingredients,
Even though it is at a cost.

Illness, frailty and disability can evoke kindness, consideration and
empathy;
These attributes are necessary for our spiritual growth,
And for our ongoing relations with one another;
Also, our limitations cause us to develop and sculpt our character;
And, whilst the natural world thrives on survival of the fittest,
Humankind has already suppressed or destroyed much of nature,
To the detriment of all, including ourselves;
Directing a portion of our attention to quality of life for all,
Provides a degree of balance,
And serves to occupy some of the surplus
Of inquisitiveness and innovation,
That carries our collective creative energy across a dangerous threshold;
From enabling progress, to madness and destruction.

Perhaps the most important ingredient of all is love:
Love, that initiated everything that is,
And that gave the gift of life-awareness,
And made the food of life itself living,
So that it would reproduce,
Enabling there always to be life;
Love makes reproduction pleasurable,

So that generations follow one another,
Perpetuating the creation of living entities;

The love that made everything, is mirrored and imitated
In our better relations with one another;
We find the young and innocent endearing,
And so they are cared for;
Finding beauty and interest in the natural world,
Is a soothing and stimulating antidote
To the pain, loss, fear and disappointment
That sometimes blight our lives;

Yes, love is the greatest ingredient of all;
Intelligence and dexterity can help us to overcome many difficulties,
But there are a great many issues,
And as many viewpoints as people;
Love drives us to stand by the vulnerable,
And to support the people and wildlife we encounter,
And the ecosystems that support us;

Love keeps going,
Because it cannot do otherwise;
It bypasses, and transcends, reason;
It does not give up on anyone,
And is our source of hope,
Whatever the state of the world.

I'm No Good with Numbers
By Patricia Griffin

4lbs 8oz -Will he live or will he die?

1 job 750 applicants – I was the one.

5 – 0 Great! Yes, but depends which side you're on.

70 in a rubber boat made for 20. 35 land and one punched in the face by
    an angry host.

£59.75. Do you split the bill on a first date?

Average house prices ten times the average salary, or for some, one tenth
    of your annual income. Go figure.

Buy one for one or three for two? Depends – Is it bleach or chocolate?

She earns much more than him, yet it is him that casts a dark shadow
    over money.

2 countries produce most of the world's wheat, and one of them ain't too
    friendly. Mmmm.

Two ex-wives and 7 children. Complicated.

In 1A.D. the world population was 2-300 million. Now it is 86 billion
    and eight people just moved in next door.

40 percent of marriages end in divorce. 60 percent don't. What does that
    mean?

17 pairs of shoes. Which pair to wear?

29 children murdered in 52 weeks. Is that normal?

Can you believe it? A bottle of water for £1.50!

10.20a.m. Two extractions - £135.00.

One lifetime, 7 cats and three dogs.

85,000miles on the clock. How many more MOTs to go?

Does £350,000m pay for a 1% pay rise?

Oh well, 4 O'clock, time for a cuppa because it's a lot to think about
    when there is only one of you.

Of Water

By Diana Newson

Plate of India, plate of Burma,
cosmic crockery crashing
the day after Christmas, and the beach
looks smaller.
The sea fizzing strangely with a head like beer.

The sea curls its lip.
We see -
what we should not see – seabed exposed.
Anemones flopped, fish gasping, graceful seaweed tendrils
        heaped.

A moment of weird quiet.

Birds fall silent and fly away.

An indrawn breath,

then people scamper down to collect fish
for tonight's tea.

All the animals on the beach
set up a low crying.
Tethered tourist mules strain inland.
From sitting, playing, I stand.

I have a moment of self-doubt.
I'm a child of ten.
All around me, adults, men,

who must know more than me –
school lessons in geography.

I speak, I say,

I think a tsunami is coming.

I think a tsunami is coming.

Inspired by Tilly Smith who saved the lives of over 100 people on her beach on the Island of Phuket, Thailand, on 26 Dec 2004. This was the day of the devasting Indian Ocean earthquake and tsunami, now known as the Sumatra-Andaman earthquake. Families fled, and no one died on her beach.

Worry at the Window

By Meher Pocha

I stand at the window

Outside people pass, busy, distracted
Children play and shout
Is that a pickpocket?

Inside, I wait

Outside there's a little commotion
An accident? An altercation?
It's hard to see

Inside, I wait

Outside the shadows lengthen
Lights come on
Front doors open and shut

Inside I wait

Why isn't he home yet?
No, I'm not annoyed
But it's time for his dinner
And he isn't back
From his dubious activities
Roaming the streets
Making unsuitable liaisons
Getting into fights

Maybe he's had an accident
Should I go look for him?
No, I'll pour myself a drink
and turn on the telly
When he gets back he'll see
I just don't care

At last a creak – he's back!
In he comes like he owns this house
Like he knows it's not mine
Stops to check what's for dinner
Settles beside me on the sofa
Curls up and goes to sleep

Why do I worry?
This happens every evening
And he's not even my cat!

Home

By Patricia Griffin

A poem is a gesture towards home
The place where love lets you in

Lets you in because you belong
Without proof of what or who you are

We are the proof of history
How far the pool of blood ran

Blood which runs and breathes still
Creating, being and climbing still

Climbing that slope of slippery barriers
Oft seeing those made to slip

But slipping through and living still
With love and joy and offering

Offering ourselves to this great universe
This place we call home where all are let in.

Forgiven

By Stephen Turner

I was present at Golgotha
And held aloft the sour-soaked sponge
To that man upon the cross
What taunting fun we had that day
When death came by that way;
Shall I ever be forgiven for that?
Dear God,
Shall I ever be forgiven for that?

I was present in the arena then,
And opened the gates for the beasts
In their den,
They tore the Christians limb from limb,
There was bone and blood,
They shrieked as they would;
Shall I ever be forgiven for that
Dear God?
Shall I ever be forgiven for that?

On Senlac hill I hacked and fought,
The Saxons fell as we knew they ought
We tricked them so they broke their ranks
And pierced them on those bloody banks;
And Harold? We so tortured him,
What taunting fun we had that day!
Shall I ever be forgiven, I pray,
Shall I *ever* be forgiven?

In Clifford's Tower we bound the Jews,
To baptise them – could they refuse?

Yet deprived we were of our desire,
They chose to start their funeral pyre!
Still, how we laughed at the crackling flames
And had such fun, such taunting fun,
Oh was it such a terrible sin?
Shall I ever be forgiven for that?
Dear God,
Shall I ever be forgiven for that?

I saw so much of awful death
That death itself was kept from me;
Thus on I lived from age to age
Such terrible things I had to see,
And enjoyed them all! How can that be?
So many horrors the years did span
Of man's inhumanity to man,
Until I found death quite unreal,
My empty heart could no more feel:
Where was my heart?
Where *was* my heart?
Shall I ever be forgiven for that?

From the Gambia coast we soon set sail
With a cargo of life, our ill-gotten gains,
Down in the bowels we could hear them wail,
There were groans, it is true, and the clanking of chains,
But soon they were still!
Why! Over the side went some who were ill!
No profit in them! But a profit we made,
Of man, woman, child in the markets of sin:
Shall I ever be forgiven for that, I prayed,
Shall I ever be forgiven for that?

My hands are not clean, can never be clean,

From the horrors I heard, the sights I have seen:
Culloden I saw, and Rorke's Drift too,
The Somme and all that, and Belsen I knew,
And that day in the east when Enola Gay flew.
Shall I ever be forgiven for that?
Oh God?
Shall I ever be forgiven for *that*?

Now here I stand
And it is time.

I shall be judged.

I have confessed.

My hands are the bloodiest hands of all,
And pleading, on my knees I fall,
Forgive me if my soul was sold,
I only did what I was told!
But God drew near with a frowning dread,
With a Mighty Roar condemned me thus:
"You are NOT forgiven!"
Was what She said.

So by Her Voice was I condemned
To live *forever*
Without end......

*[This work is to raise the question of whether, and to what extent, we can
be considered – as individuals – to be guilty of historical misdeeds.]*

Pulling on the Strings
By Erol Hasan

George entered the town square, freed his guitar from its case, and took a couple of sips of water. It was about 11.00 a.m., and there was a steady flow of people, with about half a dozen sitting on benches. The sky was mostly blue, so hopefully those with time to spare would feel inclined to stay and enjoy the sunshine. He started to play his guitar, and began singing:

> One summer day, I was walking in the sun;
> I was on my own, like a convict on the run;
> Little did I know, the real trouble had not begun;
> I was trapped, I was scared, and my life was almost done

> I am weeping,
> But I'll cry more tomorrow;
> I've been sleeping,
> Now my life is filled with sorrow;
> Rescue me, rescue me;
> O Lord, if you will.

An elderly man and woman settled on a bench…

> I wonder, if you have a someone
> Who shares in your sorrow;
> Who is here today,
> And still with you tomorrow;
> Who loves you so much
> That they will never leave;
> Until fate determines
> That one of you must grieve

A dishevelled man settled, accompanied by an elderly-looking
    mongrel dog....

My dog loves me more than I love him,
Though I sure love him a lot;
He looks out for me,
And keeps me company,
Whether I deserve it or not;
He is man's best friend,
And there's no end,
To the loyalty of my dog.

The man with the dog raised his hand in acknowledgement.

George switched to a different tune:

There are some who have talent;
They still have to work hard;
There are those who use their brains,
Like Rainman or the Bard;
Practical types, good with their hands
The charismatic and impulsive,
Who rule the lands...

"Nice" shouted a man in a leather jacket, with a laugh.
"It is nice", his mate mildly rebuked him.

George paused a few seconds, then continued:

There is no one in this world
That don't need love;
There is no one so tough,
Or made of such stuff,
That they don't need

A hand on their shoulder;
As we get older,
Our bodies slow down;
We are frightened by the energy
Of younger, fitter people,
As we cannot keep up with them;
We need LOVE
We need FAITH
We need COURAGE
We need HOPE
We need the Lord,
Each and every one of us;
Only the Lord is bigger than our troubles;
There is no other way...

His voice was breaking up. The friend of the man with the leather jacket
came over, took off his watch, and placed it in the guitar case.
"Put that in your pocket", he whispered. If times get tough, you can
pawn it." He then walked over to the man with the dog, and handed him
a couple of notes, putting his finger in front of his own mouth, to indicate
that no response was required.

"Gone soft?" shouted his mate
"You need strength to show compassion, when required; and to resist
force…when required. You'll learn."

Don't Ask Me Any Questions
By Meher Pocha

When you see me looking with vacant eyes
Wondering if I know you
Don't ask me questions
Just tell me who you are

When I forget dates and places
And insist you never told me
Don't call me stupid
Don't shout – I will still hear you
Hold me close and let us build
A new set of memories

When I keep talking of what you did
And said when you were little
But have forgotten what you said
Only five minutes ago
Don't say "How many times must I tell you?"
Just tell me again...and again

When you see me looking at the puzzle
We did together all those years ago
Anxious because the pieces don't fit
Worried they may be lost forever
Don't say, "Oh Grandma!"
Just nudge the pieces towards me

When I get lost finding the bathroom
And put shoes in the fridge
When I look at a page and wonder

If I will ever learn the patterns
That make sense of the world
Take the book and read it to me

I will by then be in the long ago
Some careless hand
Will have passed a damp sponge
Over the precious painting of my life
Leaving only smudges
With islands of clarity

So, when you see me walking in the snow
In my sun dress
Don't get cross
Throw around my shoulders
The cloak of kindness
And take me home

Winter Window

By Patricia Griffin

Trees spikey, sparse and structural
Still ground under shifting blue-grey sky
Yellow winter-flowering Jasmine
Surprises in this cool scene.

Today, all day, I will sit and consider,
Another year has passed
The happy and the quotidian
In hand with the deeply sad.

And as I sit in winter stillness
Reckoning and daring to hope
Old thoughts and
Old friends come and sit for a while
And then go.

Mandela's window
Was high up and small
Facing a concrete wall
And yet,
Even from that unpromising window
Hope came in.
So tomorrow, tomorrow,
I'll take on the world.
Well, some of it.

Balance Me

By Erol Hasan

Lord, balance me;
My right side and left;
Let neither dominate too much;
Let me not dwell too much on the past,
Or dream of a future that is unknown,
But live in the present,
Mindful that we can learn from the past,
And create a better future.
Give me enough to eat,
But do not tempt me with too much;
Give me warmth, for comfort and health,
But do not let me fall into lethargy;
Give me security and safety,
Whilst recognising the benefit of challenge;
And the usefulness of survival instinct,
In sharpening the mind and the senses,
And in developing character.
Make me trusting, where possible,
But not naïve, to the detriment of myself,
Or of any living being;
Help me to recognise right from wrong,
And the value and purpose of the law;
But also the need to challenge the rules,
As they are constructed and interpreted by mortal beings,
And subject to local and temporal bias and whim;
May I also learn from ideologies,
But not be enslaved by them;
Grant me will-power; but also
Teach me when to honourably withdraw.

Let me understand the value of victory,
But also, that an objective pursued
Must be beneficial to all,
Or, at worst, neutral.
Let me assert my ego in striving to do good,
And never at the expense of another being.
Keep my body healthy and fortified;
Let the juices that need to, flow;
Keep me fit, and able to function in this world,
So I may run to help another,
Or fight a genuine threat;
Never let me abuse my physical strength;
I need benevolence and judgment, at least in equal measure
To physical prowess.
Finally, all these things must apply to all of humanity;
And, indeed, to everything;
All living beings, our planet,
Your beautiful and wondrous universe;
Tempering humanity's rampaging success
In dominating this world.
And, to that end, give us wisdom,
In equal measure to our intelligence.
One more request:
Please do not fall out of love with us,
The way that some appear to have
Stopped loving you;
Amen.

Educating Medusa

By Diana Newson

Medusa turns men to stone.
They bend over groaning,
hiding hard-ons that take
24 hours to subside.
Medusa, Medusa, they mumble.
It's her fault they lie awake all night.

Wear more, cover up.

Wear less, no burkinis here.

Your hair isn't right Medusa.
It's wild, like non-school afro hair –
your uniform skirt is down to here,
your PE skirt is up to there.
You're still too young, it's so unfair.

Medusa was punished for her effect,
(deliberately caused, m'Lud).
There were rules she disobeyed.
And then more rules,
And then some more rules.

The charger of Perseus

breathes hot on her neck.

Under one roof

By Stephen Turner

I drew back the curtains. Would I find that a morning was there?
Yet I found not a garden, not flowers, not trees nurtured in dawn's air,
Only an unending blackness, a vacuum where none living could ever
draw breath,
The Universe I saw was not one of life, not one of hope, just the cold,
cold closure of death.

But in the rooms of my house lived many cousins, sisters and brothers,
Len was there, Diana, Paul, Meher, Heather, Patricia, Matthew, and all
of you others,
And in rooms beyond those, lived neighbours, and friends, and so too,
more distant folk,
Europeans, Asians, Africans, no matter our shade, no matter the
language we wrote, what tongue we spoke.

Yet my house was so small. So cramped! How it caused us to fight, and
to squabble,
To do battle, and to kill, to destroy as we will – and to triumph with
"victory" over some bloody rubble!
Until every corner, every nook, every cranny, with horror, with corpses,
with hate could rejoice,
The screams, and the sobs, and the shouting - they sprang at me that
morning, all with one voice.

It was a voice of the past: do not go gentle into that dark night!
Rage, rage, rage against the dying of the light!
For we are drowning not waving - why, oh, what fools we mortals be,
So when the bell tolls, remember this, and shudder, for sure it tolls for
thee.

And as it tolled, clanged at that final hour, recall that we were told!
We...were.... told!
And, through a glass darkly, found that all our cluttered souls, for fossil
fuels, were sold!

Thus out of this cacophony – might I still be sleeping, and this just a
dream?
There gradually coalesced one voice, one idea, one message, one evident
theme,
And, that very morning, I heard quite clearly that it spoke a stark truth,
This: How many rooms I had, how many tenants there, yet dwelled we
all: under one roof.

Some Dared to Think Green

By Erol Hasan

They were mocked,
And deemed crazy:
Environmentalists, pacifists,
Animal sympathisers and
CND campaigners:
Foresight, dissent and creative thinking,
Ditto compassion,
Have always been viewed with suspicion,
And treated with disdain:
In fact, anything that challenges our conscience,
And that requires discipline, and
The reining in of our appetitive instincts,
Such as religion, and philanthropic campaigning,
Is inconvenient to many,
And elevates moral courage
Over machismo and swagger.
It is unsettling, and renders the dissenting voices
An unpopular minority section;
And yet, time is proving them right:
How could the guardians, on Earth,
Of Planet Earth,
Have been careless and naïve
About the future of our natural home?
And why are we still engaging in combat,
Seeking personal and collective aggrandizement,
As the temperature rises?

Eulogy for the Goldfish

By Patricia Griffin

You came
You shone
You swam.

I loved you
You died
Damn!

The Fox-Man
By Stephen Turner

In the fox-garden
I have seen, and smelled, and heard him,
When I was out with Emm, or out with Mark,
It was, indeed, the fox-man,
Him I wish to chase - to whom I always bark.

But he is not fox,
Not one of those, that in the dark,
Stand, beyond the wire, and stare,
Their eyes a-glow,
Fascinated,
As, for my part, I growl and bark,
Unable to reach them; while full knowing that they are there.

But the fox-man
Truly understands,
And I him too;
That we are fellow creatures
Through and through;
And stretched out, sleeping, before winter's warming flames,
I dream we chase together,
Running through woods and fields,
Laughing, barking, twisting this way, that, in endless games,
My legs are twitching in my dreams,
I even growl
When some imaginary danger threatens us, it seems.

But the fox-man is old,
His hair is grey,
The time approaches when his bell be tolled,

That final day,
When, by and by,
He shall join the Great Bear, Orion, the Dog Star too,
And I discern a new star, in the sky;
Oh! The long dog days of summer shall close, shall all be through.

And in the fox-garden
There'll be no sight, no smell, no sound,
Nought for me to bark at, whichever way I bound;
And the fox-man
Sadly
Shall never there, again, be found.

The Wall

By David Strong

Staring at the wall.
Blankly.
Motionless yet cogitating mind
Always thinking, worrying, blind.
What do I think of it all?
Whilst blankly staring at the wall.

There was a worry, a pain, and fear
Sharp jabs here and here and here.
Pummelling, the knots of nothing do I feel.
Why? What does it mean? What is real?
What do I know? Nothing.
Blankly staring at a wall.

I am dying.
Not suddenly, not immediately, not now.
Not tomorrow or next week or month
But slowly, inexorably slowly;
Drifting lethargically downhill.
My confidence flares away as dark matter;
Leaking, draining and escaping.
I don't care.
I don't care.
Enough.
Gone is vitality and enthusiasm,
Gone is brightness and clarity and purpose.
Replaced and shrouded in mist
By indecision, and melancholy.

Staring at the wall.
Blankly.
Motionless yet in turmoil of mind
Always thinking, worrying, blind.
What do I think of it all?
Whilst blankly staring at the wall.

What happens when you hit the wall?
Is it sudden? Violent and inevitably life changing.
Or can it be a bouncing, soft, glancing,
Boring, boring series of collision scraping
Grinding friction to stillness and oblivion.

I often think of those that came before.
How can I not?
When their lives and memories are so entwined
Meshed and combined,
With mine.
Still part of me, still with me.
And missed.
Kind faces of those I loved
Infiltrate and invade my everyday thoughts.
They would reassure me,
And would comfort me. I know.
They know.
And I smile warmly,
Really, nothing to be afraid of
There is, one and all.
Whilst I sit blankly staring at the wall.

Walking in the Dark

(with apologies to Milton)
By Meher Pocha

So spring has come round again
I feel the unseen sun on my face
never again to see it rise or set
the scent of spring flowers fills the air

It is dark as I walk
in the summer warmth
tap-tap, tap-tap
roses – I smell the invisible roses
I can hear the cows and sheep
but most I miss beloved faces
stored in the memory

Tap-tap, tap-bump-tap
thank you, but no I don't want to cross the road

I walk into autumn – my favourite season
with the fading warmth of the mellow sun
and into the cold crunch of inevitable winter

I miss the colours as this cloud hangs over me
facing perpetual darkness
all I ask is for a strong inner light
and the clear eyes of the soul
so I might see and tell
of things invisible to mortal sight

Flora

By Erol Hasan

There is nothing
In the cupboard;
Flora has a big heart,
And a sharp mind,
But not a thing to eat;
She is poor,
Because she is not wanted;
She gave all she had,
Only to be abandoned
By the family
She had fed,
And taught her own good ways to.
Very soon, Flora's brain will slow
Due to lack of food;
And then, ditto,
That beautiful heart
Will no longer beat;
Her faraway family will appear
To reap sympathy and property.
And then Flora will be erased from memory
And conscience.

The Leaf Man
By Stephen Turner

The leaf man is in my garden again, this time of year,
It is October, the trees are sad, weeping leaves like tear on tear,
And in response the leaf man has his rake, yet never speaks;
Wrapped in himself, he has the many memories that he keeps.

To and fro, to and fro, his rake will rhythmically go,
Heaping the leaves, tear-drops from the trees gathered like banks of
    frozen snow;
But the true cold snow has still to come, to play its wintery part,
Chilled in advance, by the coldness and the desolation of the leaf man's
    heart.

He thinks – I know this – while raking rhythmically, of that frisky lass
He met and loved and married, when the spring leaves still graced the
    trees,
So many many leaf years since, and now long gone,
When he vowed to care for her, to tidy their lives – like the leaves! - as
    he has surely done.

So understanding, as I do, his thoughts, and how the leaf man grieves,
I leave him to himself, and to his weeping sweeping leaves,
Say nothing to him; accordingly he speaks not to me;
There are no words, I know, that from our grief can ever set us free.

The leaf man has gone now, he came into my hall
Where hangs a mirror, straightly raked and tidy on my wall,
And here he looked, and this is what I saw:
He and I, but one alone was standing there, and no-one more.

Window with a long view

By Diana Newson

The wishes of others, guide us for years long,
Without these signals, we just dream and daydream,
Living off people and coasting along
Slipping like fish in and out of the stream.

But following orders is burning our time,
Smoke in the stairway blocking the view,
The window opaque and covered in grime
False orders taking an age to work through.

Something self-harming in each of our souls
Made us choose the difficult road.
The self-saboteur thwarts easy goals
And chooses the heaviest thorniest load.

Yet by dumb and blind luck I end up with you.
Ships in the same harbour again and again.
We dithered forever, and said "we are through"
Before we had even begun, my dear friend.

We married, but late, tired and more worn.
The window swung open to sky on that day
A cascade of meaning breaking like dawn
And veils of distraction falling away.

Window on Self

She annoys me.
Say "She always – She never – "
but I am the same.

Freestyle

By Stephen Turner

There was an old man
Who didn't live in a shoe,
But nobody asked him
What it was he didn't do,
"I'm a poet," he said,
"And write Limericks too,
Verses, stories, indeed anything read,"
So here's an example I've written for you:

There was an old lady called Mary,
Whose face was so hollow and scary,
She took to the gin,
And committed a sin,
Threw away her razor, became hairy!

But surely, you say,
That's very old hat,
Can't you pen something else,
More modern that that?

There was a young woman called Mary
Who was rather mixed up and contrary
She took to the ale
Grafted on a new tail
Bought a new razor, became Harry!

So that sorry old man
Who lived not in a shoe,
Was well off on the whole
Was not on his uppers

But lost his own sole!
He was sadly heptagonal
In a triangular hole
And – this is his history,
A sad, tangled history:
The world was to him an unresolvable mystery!

Here is his story
From forty years since
Written one day,
Entitled "Sweet Way":

Clean curtains and the welcome mat,
But nobody came by today,
I polished up my conversation,
For the no-one that came my way,
My way,
For the no-one that came my way.

Sharpened pencils and set out pens,
A white page waiting there to say
How nice it was to see them there,
The no-one that had come my way,
My way,
The no-one that had come my way.

The flowers are dusted, spick and span,
Some new shoes, yes, I think I may,
Open the door and let them in
If no-one has arrived this way.
This way,
If no-one has arrived this way.

To no-one I address these words,

A poet's words are madness, aye,
A sharp formed madness of himself,
But saner in their own sweet way,
Sweet way,
But saner in their own sweet way.

Therefore,
Absent from his shoe,
I tell,
He was like a hermit crab
Without a shell,
And on this state
I just reflect
That he wrote his epitaph for all the world:
"Please, if I could,
I only wished to be understood"
But sadly he failed to intersect,
Like parallel lines
He

- could not connect!

And so, dear reader,
The curtain falls
On that ancient writer
Of houses without walls
On rhymes that end in a terrible muddle
And sentences that read with full-stops in the middle
On clothes that are worn, yet not on a model,
On accolades given, which are still not a medal,
….And yet he is searching
(As I'm sure that you knew)
For that comfortable, habitable, desirable shoe!

And when "they" came to cart him away
All witnessed a scene of great innocence there,
So simple a scene of such beauty and more
That was brought to an end that was ghastly to see,
And listening carefully some vowed that they heard
His lament he had struggled so long – for a word!

Epilogue

And yet, dear reader, there is still something more,
About that old man, who didn't live in a shoe,
For, in the padded cell, the life he now knew,
He listened each day to Radio 4,
And here he discovered *how* he was afflicted and sick,
He was NOT "dyslexic", nor "autistic", nor any other "-ic",
But how *tight* was he bound, his life *so* perverse!
For the answer was this:
He was simply,
Yes, simply
"Neurodiverse"!

The Tower is Tilting

By Erol Hasan

You did not exactly lie,
But allowed them to believe
Something about you
That was not true;
It suggested you to be a better person
Than you were at that moment;
You meant no harm;
You were weak -
Just for a moment;
You thought that that would be that;
But people were impressed;
The mistaken impression became
A gold crown on your head;
It got increasingly heavy,
As you were slowly being crushed
By your aggrandisement,
Based on inadequate foundations;
And 'them' increased in number,
So it was increasingly difficult to hide;
Expectations of you grew;
That was a pressure
That felt like a vice compressing your entire being;
But you appeared glorious to others,
And would be shamed, if found out;
Every time I see you,
You are more tense than before;
Your smile is less believable,
Your laugh is forced;
You are faking happiness,
And trying to appear comfortable with yourself.

You are at ease with yourself,
Or at least you could be;
But you are like a wildebeest masquerading as a lion;
You have taken more strain
Than I had ever imagined you could;
But at what cost!
And not only to yourself;
The tell-tale signs are starting to appear;
You cannot keep this up forever;
But don't panic.

Nobody is going to reject you
(For that is what we all fear most);
They may scorn the "you" they are seeing,
But it is an illusion;
What they see is an ego standing like a monument;
Tall enough to hit the ground with devastating force,
But with no chance of reaching the sky,
Let alone beyond;
Your tower of public status
Is a target that is easy to hit;
Let it fall!
Let your ego dissolve;
Open yourself to the substance of the world;
Be part of it:
No better or worse than the rest,
But an ingredient that contributes to the whole,
Because it is unique;
Be you;
Like yourself and the world;
Enjoy being, and like Being;
The pressure will drain away,
And you will not implode.

There and Back – A Story for Midsummer

By *Allison White*

A rose bud furled around its stem
Reminder of a time way back when
Midsummers sitting sipping wine
Days seemed longer way back then

The scent of Solitude wafts gently by
Rose petals glow like a sunset scene
As the sun sinks behind the clouds
There's a glimpse of life as it might have been

Memories of a swing amidst the beds
Reflecting on life as it was then
Neighbours chatting over cups of tea
Who knows where they went and when?

Sipping Rose wine, absorbing the quiet
Thoughts of how the seasons come and go
A smell, a touch, a sound, and sight
Creates the experience of life we know.

The sun has faded, light drifts from the moon
I bend to smell a rose as I did back then
As my mind recalls all my memories
I smile with gratitude for my life again

Melancholia

By David Strong

There is a clamouring inside my head;
If I let it surface.
Mostly with its roots in my past.
I see dead people.
I see places and moments and times that are gone.
But in my head the faces are still there,
Unchanged and even though it was such a long time ago,
There is an inescapable sadness about it all.
Sadness upon sadness. Mum, Dad, Brother, Friend. Dead.
And death is so final and in deliberating upon this finality
I cannot help be prodded and poked and reminded
Of my own mortality. And that can be sad.

The past is still there.
It won't go away.
I can still picture houses. 402, 400, 46, 147.
They are not just numbers.
They are memories that weigh down on me,
A heaviness of thoughts that, if I let them,
Can lead to a sloping of my shoulders and a sigh in my breath.
But it usually does not last long,
But hey! let's put a label on it.
Everything needs a label nowadays.

I saw Brian Hayes today.
But it wasn't him.
He was in my life 25 years ago.
I thought of Joannie Root (I bet she didn't spell her name like that)
She was from 40 years ago.
Photographs. Holidays from decades ago.

And, yes, happy memories. But that is all that they are.
Those days don't come back. And that is so sad.
Sadness upon sadness.

Songs do it to me too. I heard Jean Genie on the radio today and very,
     very happy times come back.
 But they are gone. They won't return. How can I still enjoy, cherish and
     appreciate something that so tangibly will never come back again.
     And I miss it.
And it's in these times, these melancholic moments. And they are
     transitory. But I do, I think of mortality.... and just a little bit, but
     enough of a bit to be measurable.
Just a bit..... I look forward to and welcome a time when the clamouring
     will stop. And it will. That sadness upon sadness will go away and
     there will be, just a bit, a release and a relief that it is gone forever.

Take My Hand

By Lionel Sullivan

Take my hand and we'll sail away
From our land of old happiness and new sorrow
To our promised future,
Where life will be better tomorrow and tomorrow and tomorrow.

Take my hand as we watch all we've ever known
Slip away in the wake of the beast of the sea,
Crying our tears for what we know we've lost
And all we hope to be.

Take my hand as we doze on our cramped bed
Escaping the hunger we feel,
Lying in each other's arms
Waiting 'til our dreams are real.

Take my hand as we push through the throng
Scrabbling and clawing with the other lost souls
Fighting for the chance of life,
Tasting the fear, the anger and the bitter, bitter cold.

Let go my hand as I push you away
Forcing you to take the chance to live
As I stay, taking my place,
And the ship starts to sink.

He Tries Writing a Sonnet in the Pub

By Paul Green

Tanked on the carbohydrate of cheap booze
the chatter-boxing influencers at the bar
curate their lives, their loves, their private views
on platform shoes or Elon's latest car
These icons self-invent, they fake their news
about the dramas where they briefly star
some car-park ruck where banter lit the fuse
when lads and ladies took a joke too far
But who am I, a hypocrite, a liar
who falsifies the world to fit his dream
my poems smell like ancient pants on fire
life's not a gift, it's just a pyramid scheme
And all our atoms tremble with the light
I'm just a proton, passing through the night

Her Rage Flew Out

By Meher Pocha

Her rage flew out in letters
Written with a red hot pen
Righting wrongs and
Supporting the unfortunate
Who came for sympathy
And went away with hope

Her rage flew out at the little Hitlers
Of bureaucracy
Causing misery and lining their pockets
Would they manage to escape
When she was after them?

Her rage flew out in action
Meeting, planning, succeeding
Inspiring others to join in saving
Open spaces to swing a bat
Or fighting for the defenceless

Her rage flew out
In modern dance
The free and forceful movements
Bringing release

When sorrow drove her to poetry
Her rage flew out in humour and satire
Shining a light
On absurdity, hypocrisy, prejudice

She fought the good fight all her life
So what would she do if she was here today
In a world seemingly gone mad
Tearing itself apart
Darkened by hate and injustice
Bent on destroying itself?

Would she despair and weep?
Maybe take up knitting?
No, she would probably burst forth
Like a giant firework
A thousand bright sparks
Breaking out in a new generation
Fighting for a better future

The Eyes are the Window
By Erol Hasan

Look at Lisa
If you can;
I can't.
She is pretty, but
There is something that makes me uncomfortable:
Her behaviour is not extraordinary;
She doesn't say anything strange;
A part of me finds her intriguing:
Yet something tells me to keep a distance;
I don't know what it is;
I'd have no idea
How to draw or describe this quality;
But it's in her eyes:
It is always the eyes.

Style

By Diana Newson

Style is clothes.
Dresses, shop-by-fit, accessorise and trend.
Fleece-back, zip-through.
Show 40 more, we'll recommend

Slider, chunky platform, buckle strap.
FOR SALE: BODYCON.
And Mini Midi Maxi wrap.

Cream short puffer gilet, and we swear
upon the party, smock and little black.
Quite nice with lace-up thigh-high pointy toes
Hair - claw, clip, and barrette it back.

Lounge, beach and swimwear, this-year-bolder.
FOR SALE: CO ORD SETS.
Ruched, base, event, and off-the-shoulder.

Slouchy, pom-pom, fluffy frilly teddy knits
are wardrobe staples, or Occasion Kits.
TEAM WITH rectangle, tote, croc chain and box,
wide white pleather, bandana, freestyle socks.

This will transform the dullest outfit.
FOR SALE: SHACKET.
Seems expensive - do not doubt it.

All these words were gathered from a single website and randomised to make a poem. And there were plenty more words…!

The Reckoning

By Lionel Sullivan

And I told you you'd regret it,
That it would come back to haunt you
That there'd be nights when there'd be screams in your dreams
When you realise what you've done.

It was the way you got inside my head
With all the words of love you said
And made me mad, made me sad and turned me bad

So this is how it has to be
And it's going to hurt you more than it hurts me.

This is the cost of what you do.

Inner Stories

By Meher Pocha

I looked at the moon
Longing with childish eyes
I knew I could have her to keep
If I tried enough and was good
For did she not follow me home
In the evening
And seem to be my friend?
But she laughed as I reached out to catch her
And broke into a thousand points of shining water

I looked at the earth
Confident it could be mine
With patience and toil
I would have the fields and rivers
The honours and prizes
But signs and warnings kept me out
And sent me away defeated

I looked at your heart and was afraid
Surely it could not be mine
For some little part long given away and forgotten
Might grow to fill it up with old loves
And dreams unfulfilled
Would I then see it slip through my fingers
Or be kept outside with angry signs?

Shaken I turned away for safety
But you gave it to me with a smile and gentleness

Happy and fearful I placed it beside me
And it stayed

Now I look sometimes at the moon and the earth
With longing
I look for your inner stories to make them mine
But I lean softly against you
And am content

The Wall

By Patricia Griffin

Our old street,
top of the alley.
Come one, come all –
Just bring your ball.

In our space
We had the odd row,
A to-do, a spat
But come the next day
We'd forgotten all that.

Hopscotch and skipping
Football, one on one.
Playing out late
Till everyone had gone.

Then later came the big uns
Like Tony's brother,
Smoking one fag
and then another.

Next day the same.
Wonder who's there?
Simon and Joe
And their sister Claire.

Got to go now
Sandwiches for tea
What are you having Shazaan?
Just dinner, Don't ask me.

The wall didn't divide us
It kept us together
Learning to live
Through all kinds of weather.

When Rosie's Mum died
And the black car came
We stood silent and looked on
Would we ever be the same?

Time passed,
And the holidays arrived.
A new family moved in
With a boy named Jim,
Didn't take long
For him to fit right in.

I don't know whether
the wall still stands
Probably bulldozed
At the corporation's hand.

Was on a bus the other day,
Saw a wall
with a sign saying,
'No Ball Games Allowed'.
Pity.

Sleep

By Diana Newson

You sleep deeply, almost concussed.
A dreamer and sleep talker, that can't be waked.
Your dive to the ocean floor is direct and quick.
You retreat far and still, dwindled into the distance,
with a vampire's protective reflex.

My sleep a tattered skein crawling across
the face of the moon. Ragged holes half-full of mantras,
breathing exercises, dog-ends of prayers.
I struggle to close doors against clamour,
and must endure each long feverish night.

I've disturbed you.
You reach out, unwoken,
and speak in a dream voice,

"Don't worry darling, everything's alright."

The Stone on the Hill

By Stephen Turner

Do you know what is in a bra?
I asked an old man, sitting by the road,
He looked beyond me, and to a hill that stood afar,
And indicated, with his hand, a stone that on the skyline showed.

But spoke he not.

And are there *chemicals* in a bra? I asked the old man where he sat,
Elastic perhaps, synthetic rubbers, treatments in the fabric too?
And can you tell me, hand on heart, that *totally* safe is <u>all</u> of that?
Fully tested, fully cleared: beyond the *slightest* doubt, can *such* be true?

But spoke he not.

Which woman wore the first-made bra; when *was* that day?
My grandmother? Her grandmother? Indeed, how long ago?
For Eve, and all her daughters, never wore a bra, I say,
Did *they* have cancer, of the breast, so commonly, as today we know?

But spoke he not.

And wore them sixteen hours a day, seven days a week, and all the year,
With all that treated stuff, those chemicals, bound firmly, deeply on their
    sweated skin?
So that, *infused* they were, *exposed* they were, *experimented on*, they
    were!
For the sake of "beauty" and of "fashion", as *men* desired, day out, day
    in?

But spoke he not.

And when a cancer formed, as if by *chance* it would,
Was there no *cause*, no molecular change, no fundamental *basis* to its
     life?
Other than pure *accident*, conjured out of thin air - as if it could!
As though a bloody stabbing death arose so painfully without the
     intervention of a knife!

But spoke he not.

And so. And so. Silent, by the road *I* fell,
For I had nothing further, nothing further still to add,
What else was there, of this dread question, for me to tell?
Except to seek a double-blind trial – of whether bras were good, or bad!?

Yet at last he spoke!

"You see that stone, there, standing on yon hill."
He pointed with his hand, and there I turned my eye,
"My wife with breast cancer became so dreadfully weak and ill,
Beyond my capability ever to help her; just to see her die."
And here he sighed.
"I cannot give you answers to what you ask,
For I know them not."
He paused, then: "this was my *only* final task,
To bury her, to weep for her, to abandon her for ever in yon plot."

I went my way, I had to live!
Wondering whether the sin was *mine*, or *his*, that neither of us, upon this
     topic, had any *warning*, usefully, to give.

Chores

By Paul Green

our local star shines through the contrails
today's morning is blue
wheezing geezer next door
exhorts his dog to piss
I am really struggling with this washing line
the shirts flap their damp paws
a nuisance call awaits me
just breathe at them with your fumes

Dalston

By Diana Newson

Driving down the Willian Road,
I always think of Dalston.
Left and right fields leap away,
Hedgerow, copse, and farmyard track.

In Dalston, you drive
on a tight chessboard of traffic.
Blocked by a stubborn pawn, a rook swoops out;
its flight spells
Check! for me.
I wait -
I hurry -
I'm skirting round -
on the groaning earth of Dalston.

Driving down the Willian Road,
quickening routes through lacy green,
summer air and blackbird song.

Happy on the Willian Road,
but I always think of Dalston.

Claiming the Wall
By Erol Hasan

Peter was not a sociable type;
He did not fit in with the crowd;
He strived hard to earn
The approval of his peers,
But they were not impressed,
By a personality that had been
Dismantled and then reassembled.
He got nervous, and stammered,
And found himself excluded from conversations;
He had a curious and agile mind;
But, deprived of opportunity
To share his ideas with other people,
His thinking became confused and complicated,
And occasionally extreme.
He was, consequently, further ostracised by his peers,
And believed that he could never
Sustain a romantic relationship,
Though this presumption was inaccurate.
He craved entry to the theatre of mainstream life,
But the wall of difficulty that impeded him
Became more sturdy and seemingly impenetrable;
Fear of further rejection turned to paranoia;
The harder he strived to conquer the wall,
The more formidable it became,
And fatigue robbed him of the belief
That he could ever flourish in this life.
With his resolve floundering,
His body weakened;
He became ill.
He lost all aspiration in life,

But clung to the will to remain alive;
He could not continue solely via his own efforts,
He needed the support of others;
In his dysfunction, he found that
There were good people who valued him,
And that he was more resourceful
Than he had imagined.
His lifetime of struggle,
Albeit frequently misdirected
And rarely acknowledged,
Had prepared him for this time,
And was testimony to his resilience:
Why should anything defeat him now?
It was reasonable to think that
He could accept any burden,
And still find moments of joy;
He could cherish these moments,
And relive them in his mind,
As often as he wished.
Life now felt light,
And the wall was no longer menacing,
But possessed kaleidoscopic beauty;
He could climb it at will,
And welcome others to his side;
The challenges of physical life
Had rendered him blind
To the beauty and radiance of his soul -
Qualities characteristic of the life-space he inhabited;
It had taken the disabling of his body
To release the liberating and enlightening spirit;
The two were now in sync,
His life harmonious;
And his body, now functional,
Facilitated a new adventurous experience of life.

Van Gogh – A Life

By Patricia Griffin

Poor Van Gogh
With his ear half off,
a rumbly tummy
and a broken heart.
He so wanted the world
to appreciate his art.

Do Not Assume

By Erol Hasan

If you insult me,
Don't assume that I won't retaliate,
Or, perhaps, take out my frustration
On an undeserving other person;
If you kick or punch me,
I may strike back,
Or assault an innocent third party;
If you gossip, in secret, about someone to me,
Don't assume that I won't circulate the story;
If you drive aggressively on the road,
Expect that others may do the same;
And if you get angry, beware!
You are not alone in having a temper;
If you gang up against someone,
Assume that your enemy will also seek allies;
And if you try to gain an advantage on another,
Through superior weapons, propaganda or cunning,
You know that your adversary will do the same.
And, so, drip by drip,
A spark of malice
Can lead to a world at war.

Evergreen Eddy

By Meher Pocha

At five our Eddy went to school
Tearful but not a fool
Learnt to read and write and spell
Till he could do them very well
Green eyes, glasses, orange hair
Bully fodder – he didn't care
Expected the world to be just and fair
It wasn't

With praise and prizes got a place
At University and could chase
Libraries and learning of his dreams
Others just saw his tattered seams
He fell for every jaded joke
Felt a fool each time he spoke
They thought they had his spirit broke
They hadn't

Put heart and soul into his work
Working for a slimy jerk
Honesty he saw they lacked
But when he spoke up he was sacked
They said the villain he should sue
He's at fault, they said, not you
Make sure he gets all that he's due
He couldn't

In wide green fields he solace found
And his beloved Angelina Pound
The green-eyed monster saw them there

And brought them discord, doubt, despair
Would they always shout and fight
Over who was in the right
Sleepless through the long dark night
They didn't

As greengrocer he earned a living
Always smiling always giving
Find a better job they said
How else will you get ahead
He didn't care, enjoyed his life
Contentment, laughter, lack of strife
Carving toys with pocket knife
He wouldn't

All things green he loved to grow
Unruly little ones in tow
With them he was a child again
Mud and Ribena, just a stain
He threw them high into the air
It seemed he didn't have a care
They thought he always would be there
He wasn't

The green grass grows above his head
The rich dark earth his final bed
But in their hearts he isn't dead

The Calm Transference of Life

By Erol Hasan

The bird of prey is neither clumsy nor angry;
It is not stupid;
It flies with grace and beauty,
And has enviable concentration and awareness;
It locates its meal-to-be,
Then swoops and kills:
It can feed its family.

The cat stalks its intended victim;
It is stronger and faster,
Stealthier, and probably more intelligent,
Than the other, hapless, creature,
Whose only option is to avoid the cat.

In a struggle, a fight,
The one who keeps control prevails;
He, who is not perturbed by emotion,
Evades the blows from his fellow combatant,
Then delivers the coup-de-grâce;
Nobility does not win the day,
However, we might wish that it did.

Cruelty and inequality do not seem to allude
To a God that cares;
To life that is blessed with mercy:
Yet, in spite of our tribulations,
And in disregard of our fear and anger,
The sun shines;
The rose blossoms;

The butterfly dances through the air;
Life is beautiful, in all its essence;
It proliferates, with nascent symmetry and elemental perfection;
Like a kaleidoscope that turns continuously,
And whose dimension, reach and beauty know no bounds.

Life entwines with death,
In a miraculous cycle;
All who catch the breath of life, do so
Against remarkable odds, and are
Constructed with mind-blowing ingenuity,
And saturated with selfless love.

Time

By Stephen Turner

On hearing part of Messiaen's "Quartet for the End of Time"

Time,
What did Messiaen think
When taken by the Germans
To Stalag VIII-A,
There to reside
Tausend Jahre!
There to compose, and play,
His quartet for the end of time!

Das Dritte Reich!
It lasted not a thousand years,
And say what you like,
It was assuredly outlived by Messiaen's timeless score.

Played first on old and well-worn instruments,
Perhaps as I heard it played on an ancient, but wonderful, cello,
Staves, bars, speaking of his melancholy, a melancholy timelessly deep,
So that, in hearing it played, I could – with sympathy, and horror - only
      weep.

Time,
Do you speak the same to me?
Travelling at an irreversible pace:
Not going back; not along the road not taken, to see
Whether the other path led to a better place,
To a better view,
To a life any happier than the happy, long life I led with you.

And time did for us all, in the end,
Did for you, my love, as it will, in turn, do for me,
For this is true: there is no end to time, my long lost lover, my wife, my
      friend;
Where, sadly, much else ceases, time goes on full endlessly.

And what is therefore also true: despite Herr Hitler's blood and gore,
Despite the horrors of the camps, the ovens, and the war,
And of Messiaen's fear, perhaps, that his belovèd wife he'd see no more,
This can be said: that Time, and Art, and Love – I see these shall endure.

Riverford Organic Veg Delivery

By Diana Newson

I must not waste, and must use up, while fresh and tasty
all the vegetables, salads and herbs they sent me.
Shallot tartlets take half a day.
Sweet potato gratin -
time-consuming and only ever a side.
Spiced lentils freighted with grated carrot,
and celery soup, hours of just celery for company.

Vegetables come straight from God
and the planet,
with that mark of sanctity that is soil.
Leaves are especially holy being made of light.
Kale, cabbage, collards and spring greens,
Spinach, chard, pak choi, and salad leaves,
which all arrive same day, to be used straight away.

I choose these hours in the kitchen and have
developed a mythology. I have a pantheon of veg.
Each speaks in its own voice and vies for the pot.
Each has a place in the calendar,
and always too many of us at the party.
I show my poem to Mum, she says

watercress?

Ubi Sunt?

By Paul Green

Where oh where are the lost planets
spinning into vortices
voids of black lightning
those orbs populated by ghosts
their monorails became webs of rust
and in the crystalline sands
claw prints of entire species faded
All art is repressed elegy
for throes of rending metal
or a child's spade half hidden
or tapes flaking into oxides
yellowing daguerrotypes
torn creases of birth certificates
where is the rubbish of times passed
in the lost worlds
abandoned domes of discovery
lands filled with rubbish
we've lost and loved.
Where is the enormous room of the night sky?
Its contractions have collapsed our wave function
The code books for those secret equations lost
like a toy railway or the book of the green elephant
and where is the Time Machine?
- lying in the mud outside marble ruins
its handlebars twisted like old fingernails

Patterns 2

By Stephen Turner

What shall we speak of now, my lovely, lovely lass?
Shall we speak, as we did, lying on the sun-patterned, dappled grass?
Of a future we might have, each piece balanced, in its ordained spot?
Balanced by texture, by shade, by sheen – better balanced, we thought,
    than not.

Place *this* shape here – and place *this* shape too,
See! The clouds pass above us – giving us their character and, we agree,
    their hue,
Of all this we spoke: what a pattern – passion permitting - we might
    build!
We reached out, touched hands; crystallised hope! Found this: our
    canvas full-filled.

Now, in a gallery – it is a *virtual* gallery, you understand - hangs the
    pattern we drew,
It *is* what we spoke of, lying where leaves patterned the sunlight, on me,
    and on you,
In a quiet corner it now hangs; many come seeking masterpieces – and
    many pass by,
But we can be proud of the picture we painted, my lovely lass, you and I.

Echoes. There are only echoes, now, of the patterned words that were
    spoken,
Faint are they, dying away, silent, I say; the brushes and palette cast
    down and broken,
Yet the sun dances still where our wishes were made - made and truly
    came to pass,
What shall we speak of now, my lovely, lovely lass?

Seeing God

By Erol Hasan

I cannot describe or explain God;
He is not visible to me,
And prevails over my ability to
Construct or determine an identity.
But it would be wrong to say
That I have no understanding of God:
The world, its people,
My own self;
The things that exist,
And our own creative tendency;
In particular, music,
With its unique spiritual quality;
Also, the unboundedness of matter, and of
That which can be perceived or conceptualized,
Both in the large and small sense,
Plus the laws of physics,
The teaching of prophets,
And the example of great people,
Both celebrated and humble:
All these, and much more,
Give a rich, albeit emerging,
Impression of God,
That does not depend on
The mental construct in our mind's eye.

Rescue Hen

By Diana Newson

There's sun here, and also night here. Birds roost at night,
on perches. (Her feet have always been
flat on the barn floor.) There's the nest box.
I put her inside, private with soft hay.
She's lived in a fever of push peck shove.
There are just two quiet sisters here,
They stick together, but she chased a fly

and ran 10 steps into wide open space.

Learning to forage, her muscles are weak.
Learning to nest, her feathers rubbed off,
but she's ready

for the first day as a chicken.

Ukraine

By *Stephen Turner*

In my orchard the crows are perched, while some sing sweetly as they
    crowd the skies,
They sing of corpses they dream they pecked, their choicest part:
    unseeing eyes,
Yet in my orchard as it stands, there are no corpses, nor choicest parts on
    which to feast,
I know they heard this awful song, and learnt it, from their cousins in the
    east.

Oh, black ragged wings: that flap and rage,
Your dreadful song, contaminates this world, echoes the mad man of our
    age,
That mad man in the east who, when the newly dead rise pleading from
    their graves,
Laughs! And nonetheless fights on, spitting blood and guts: and, yes, so
    wantonly he raves.

But now I hear that crows can sing no more.
They only cackle like the sound of grinding tracks, like the stuttered
    machine guns of this war,
And as the shrapnel – and the sundered bits – fall from the sky
The keen crows settle: to feast, to argue, to fight upon the corpse's
    unseeing, choicest eye.

The unseeing eye: why, once it saw!
It saw the yellow corn fields, the blue sky up above, the beauty of some
    lovely girl, the darkling eve, and so much more,

It saw a future, a place of hope, where men and women could kindly
tread: and would be free!
Until one vivid flash, that metallic sliver, that termination of the choicest
eye, and its ability miraculously to see.

Now, in my orchard, there is perched a mighty army of those silent
crows,
Silently they tell me of the eastern war, of all their suffering, of all their
loss, and all their woes,
They stand as auguries, and silently they say:
Take note, for soon the wind of death may find you too; hear us! shall
most assuredly come this way.

Night falls, hides the silent crows and, in an almost-peace, lovingly the
sleeping land enfolds,
I am not a prophet! I know indeed what I may wish. But, dear Ukraine,
my little orchard too, I can but dimly see, to sketch out what a
future holds.

Saying "No" to War

By Erol Hasan

Lord, tell them to stop:
They make excuses, blame one another;
But still they seek to win,
By hurting their adversary
More than the reverse;
They are not agents of God;
They are not motivated by any virtue;
Nor are they patriots,
In any decent sense of the word;
They are killers, plain and simple;
Doing what they want to do:
And, as long as we are too scared to say "no more",
They will continue the carnage.

Evergreen
By Meher Pocha

green eyes orange hair glasses
bully fodder
bruises, bumps, practical jokes
the lonely playground
resilience
scholarship
university
apple pie bed
involuntary river-dips
green walks
solitude
it is as it is

success
green shoots of hope
workophile
whistle-blower
job drought
no matter

love at last
stalked
green-eyed monster
nibbling away
survive
thrive

greengrocer
really?
green beans
greengages
green fingers
friend
fireside philosopher
grandpa
stories
football
songs
sticky hands
hide and seek
laughter

under green grass
tears
eulogies
still alive
in memoriam

Travelling but Never Arriving

By Diana Newson

I played in a previous life – saw it in a dream.
In my heart I know I can play,
I expect to be able to play,
but faced with strings, frets, notes on a stave -
I plink, I plonk, I twang tuneless.

I picked up the instructions again,
(the words are familiar friends).
I'll tune it and learn all notes again -
but they sound too different, or samey,
although both C, both D, both E.

I picked up some tunes again,
the music a painful translation,
when it used to be so toot sweet.
I want to get to new settings but only travel
these everyday commonplace plains.

I've run out of time again,
of commitment and motivation.
I never practice enough to be good,
and never good enough to carry on.
Next year I start from scratch, again.

Kora Man

By *Patricia Griffin*

You enchanted me
that Gambian night
Sitting in your golden robe
Leading
heavenly notes from
your Kora to my heart.

Alphabet

By Stephen Turner

I awoke. The room was oh! so dark, the night not done!
And like some scuttering mercury that – in globules – ran away,
I found that sleep had fled, was in that moment gone,
And in that instant, my wakened mind was fully clear - like day;
I tossed about, the unborn poem still an empty page.
Minutes passed; nor sleep nor words I found,
It seemed a lifetime, and an endless age,
Anxiety and distress, only these went round and round,
And, what is worse,
Yet nothing of them formed a verse.

I lay abed, the dark so infinitely deep with gloom,
Nothing could I see of it, nor rug, nor shelf - just feel an endless, wall-
    less room,
And utter still. I sighed, as though this sound would hopefully conjure
    thought,
That sigh! I started! Was that an echoing sigh it brought?!
But then a chuckle, deeply throated, I distinctly heard,
Quite near! My hair rose on my head,
For, and I was sure, this nearby Voice now whispered word on word,
And, to my utmost horror, this is what it said:

"You fool! You struggle to write some lines.
Your mind is empty, oh you feeble thing,
Where is your power to forge some alphabetic signs,
To give them meaning, to make them speak, to make them sing,
When so many symbols – twenty-six I say!
Are at your hand!

And yet - this endless night - no matter how you pray,
You can not pen a verse the world may ever understand."

And on it spoke:
"So all of Shakespeare, Milton, Donne, and who you would,
Why! Praise Hemingway, the Brontes, Austin – and all those *prosing*
    folk,
Who, from that alphabet, made much – as much they could!
Yet none that breathed, or loved, or moved, or even thought!
But lifeless on a page it lay
As dead as nails! All twenty-six of breathless ink
Never breathed a second, a minute, one hour, one day,
And of itself could never laugh, or cry, or dream, or even think!

So in the gloom, this Voice expressed its scorn
While on the bed lay I, my muse so lacerated, failed, and torn.

And yet the Voice said, wounding like a knife:
"You useless thing! How weak you are and poor!
I made the world, and on it so *diverse* a life,
And for this life, of letters I used only *four*!
From these – you call them A and T and C and G,
I made the lowest things, the bugs, the bears, the greatest of them all,
The plants, the lichens, bushes, briars, the tallest tree,
The crab, the whale, and all those fishes in the sea,
Amazing in their forms, their vast diversity,
For *all* of these, on only symbols *four* did I make call!
And with these four, wrote myriad *living* novels, odes, and let them run,
I made *all* thriving things, and gave them breath,
So they were born, and grew, and prospered in the sun,
Sentenced they were, and – yes – full-stopped in death!

So spoke the Voice; of this I'm sure,
The last it spoke, it whispered just this word. The word was "four!"

And now the room was empty, save only me,
The Voice was gone, and in the dark I knew that I could see,
And what I saw with blinding certainty was this,
That twenty-six was both too much, and not enough,
That whatever I wrote - however great - I'd miss
A creation so wondrous, so subtle, soft, amazing, yet so tough,
As four letters wrote in making life on Earth,
An alphabet so small that nonetheless spelled "life", and "love" and, yes,
    spelled "birth"!

Courage

By Erol Hasan

In order to walk,
We must risk falling;
We form and maintain friendships,
Accepting the possibility of rejection or treachery;
And exercise our body and improve our physique,
Tolerating the likelihood of incurring injury,
At some point in time.

When we think logically for long periods,
We may get tired and tense;
And creative thinking,
So vital to a healthy mind,
To progressive thinking and to advancement,
Paradoxically can lead to a loosening of our hold on sanity.

All these things are better performed "in the present",
Without the burden of active contemplation;
Danger can be acknowledged,
But then, where appropriate, accepted
As part of the yin-and-yang,
Rollercoaster-ride nature of attaining rewards;

It is in a medium of uncertainty
That we develop our character,
And that we define and illuminate our personality,
Thus giving purpose to our life.

If we do not have faith in the loving benevolence of life,
We shall clutch desperately to a contracting world of security;
If we have learned, from our experiences,
To mistrust people,
We shall be prone to mutual rejection,
Unwilling to commit to anyone;
We can distance ourselves sufficiently,
In order not to dissolve in love for another;
But then reflection on one's isolation
Is a form of generalised grieving;
It is exacerbated by the absence of memories,
That might punctuate and illuminate
The abyss of loneliness.

All the Little Animals

By *Stephen Turner*

Round and round they go,
Scuttering, scrabbling, scampering: in this way have they sped
All the little animals
That nibble in my head;
So much have they thus nibbled me, so much have they thus fed,
Both from above, and from beneath,
How much that's left is void, I ask, and how much left is truth?

What sharp and biting teeth they have,
And scratching, knife-edged claws,
And bright eyes, gleaming red they have,
And clamping squirrelled jaws,
What clumsy, clumping routes they passed,
With miners' boots upon their paws:
How can I sleep? How can I think? How can I rest?
My head so full of little animals, and their pestilential wars!

Round and round they go,
Scuttering, scrabbling, scampering: like sparrows in my loft,
Never a moment's peace I know,
My mind with tumbling torrential torment stuffed,
My Thames tide turning tightly, with torturing ebb and flow,
Through my doors, and through my windows - in, and then straight out,
Their twitching noses, and their whiskers, the little animals show,
What! For God's sake leave me! In peace, please leave me – is what I
    shout.

And so,
Peace will!

And all the little animals, that 'habited my head,
Are suddenly quite still.
Silence in the void! – there is little left of truth,
There's so little left for them to nibble, above or, yes, beneath,
And yet the dreaded stillness is so pregnant with "Beware!"
Beware! Beware! Beware!
For all the little animals – you can be very sure – are quiet indeed – and
    yet they are still there!

Those Who Cannot Speak

By *Erol Hasan*

With no power to change
Their condition or circumstance,
They get through the days and nights;
They cannot hurt or help anyone,
Except by transmitting joy or sorrow
Through facial expression
Or evocative outcry;
Yet they find a reason to go on,
And a way to communicate,
And the will to endure
Whatever life brings;
They appear to have so little,
But they value what they have;
Some cannot control their bodies,
Yet, through their honesty and self-tolerance,
Retain their dignity.

Few would have the courage
To swap places, if it were possible;
But, through their daily struggles,
They have acquired fortitude
That would benefit any living being.

Really Enjoy a Hand-made Christmas

By Diana Newson

I plan to hand-make Christmas,
starting in November.
This year I'll make a bûche de noel,
and handcraft all my cards.
I've found 3 new gold reindeer for the tree
which only need a bit of gluing.
There's the cake, the pudding…the Christmas veg,
The Lights Switch On, and the Christmas tree festival.

Reality dawns -
I've not made it to the Carol Service
for the last 20-odd years.
Along with dogs, cats and hedgehogs,
I hate all fireworks and bonfires.
I hate saying thank you for weird presents
that get filed under "B" for bin,
and making stollen takes about 2 days full-time.

And then to cap it all, YOUR MOTHER

Oh, for God's sake - just buy it all.

Many Ingredients

By Stephen Turner

Foreword

It was a Greek
Standing by the Aegean,
Or was it a Persian
Who gave it creation?
Or, perhaps, in that ancient pandemonium
It was a Babylonian
Who was quite certain
That the prime ingredients oughta
Be Air, Earth, Fire, and Water!

Air

I have heard you, I have felt you,
I have sensed the wind a-blowing,
Yet no-one saw you, no-one knew
That atoms moved the leaves a-soughing;
And in my ancient book of "physick",
Where the heart was already known: a pump,
The purpose of the lungs was "mystic",
For – poor Lavoisier! – the guillotine had left his neck a stump!
His "oxygen" only known to few,
Therefore the wind anonymously blew,
Oh Air! How can anyone, in ancient times, have comprehended you?!

Earth

I stand on you, my legs placed firmly and apart,
You are so very solid, fashioned from an ancient rock,

You feel so still! Yet through the heavens, like some primaeval dart,
You dash! Dash around the sun, and back,
And yet! And yet in ancient days,
The Earth was central, imperious, so the old believe,
It was the sun that ran the race,
A chariot hastening in the sky from morn to eve,
Across the heavens. Earth! Earth! You are my source,
I am made from you, born of you,
And this I vow,
In you I slumber when I have run my narrow, bitter course.

Fire

Those rocks, left in the redded fire,
Ran metal from their broken souls,
Copper, tin - then did conspire
To shed iron: spears, swords, and ploughing tools,
Envisioned in the minds of those
Rough hands and limbs that gave them breath,
Breath from the bellows – whose actions chose
To fashion ploughshares into tools of death!
Oh Fire, Fire, from whence came you?
Why, from the sunlight, shining on the tree!
And this is true:
The wooded sunlight trapped, the ancients found: then carelessly they set
    it free.

Water

Finally – can this be all the ingredients that there really are?
Across a desert I drag myself,
Parched – parched from life, devoid of love, my skin so burnt, so torn, so
    bare,
Needing Water to revive an instinctive wish for life;

And yet note this: of all the miracles water is the most,
Changing density as it turns to ice,
A solid less dense! Thus floats! And forms a "skin",
Protecting all the aqueous creatures that live in this space,
Until the warmth of spring releases them therein,
To swim, to breed, to crawl, evolve, upon some sandy coast,
A backbone, four fins, toothed and bony jaws,
Turning, eons onwards, by some Darwinian laws,
Into man!
And if they can:
Perhaps also to that very sapient Greek upon Aegean shores?

Epilogue

Some said there was a fifth ingredient, and that its name
Was Aether. Quintessence! But still time passed, and yes!
Amongst the Cumbrian hills, a man called Dalton came,
Took up the Greeks' ideas: of atoms! And then, I guess,
Gave them form, little symbols, and even names!
And found, with study, that two hydrogens combined and formed,
With one oxygen: water! And by these intellectual games
Passed on, to Mendeleev, the fundamental secret of it all: and so defined
The ingredients of everything! Air, Earth, Water. But yet of Fire,
They found that heat was energy, not matter. 'Til Einstein said
That matter is but frozen energy: "e" equals "m" "c" squared!

And so (as if I cared):
How much do we owe to that sapient Greek, you may enquire,
Or is it a Persian, or Babylonian, to whom we come?
Bringing the final ingredients of our doom:
The thermonuclear *fission*, or so much worse, the *fusion* bomb!

The Unconditional Love of a Pet

By *Erol Hasan*

It does not judge,
And is quick to forgive;
It rarely rejects affection,
And does not assert an ego;
It is loyal and patient,
And demands little from us:
However considerate we are,
Our pet will inevitably
Treat us in a better way
Than we act towards it,
As it is humble and naively trusting:
The environment we have created
Is for our convenience,
And a cat or dog must fit in;
Although there are some rogues,
Most people do love their pet;
But rarely as much as the pet loves us.

Mango
By Patricia Griffin

How to eat a mango?
Messily, with gusto
And full – bodied enjoyment.

Where to eat a mango?
In a hot place with
Warm family on
Solid ground.

When to eat a mango?
When they are in season
and the mango tree
looks like paradise itself
and it seems as if
this time will never end.

Reckoning

By Stephen Turner

Arriving at The Pearly Gates, as was my due,
I met St. Peter, and this is true,
I said: suppose I was a Muslim, Hindu, Buddhist, or a Jew?
And He replied: why, then this Entry Point is not for you,
Go over there, and join a different Queue.

I stood my ground for plain-speaking was my way,
Look, I said, You can not "reckon" me on this, or any other day,
For, on the contrary, I stand here so I may "reckon" You,
You, and All Those within the Pearly Gates, for what You do,
Where was Your mercy, Your kindness, Your omnipotent power,
Your help, Your sympathy – Your love! – in life's most needful hour?!

But St. Peter, at this, He looked right sorely vexed,
And in His most dismissive voice He called out "Next!"
But still I stood my ground, would not be moved,
For I had sat beside the bed of her I loved,
The bed we slept so happily together in, for years and years gone by,
And where, latterly, I saw her suffer – suffer undeservedly – and saw her
    die.

I said: You take Your reckoning and stuff it where You may!
I'll have none of Your nonsense, of after-life eternal. For this I say:
I know that Those inside the Pearly Gates climbed over heaps of souls:
Dead Christians, Unbelievers – many! – to reach Their heavenly goals,
And so, of this You can be very sure,
I'll wait not in Your Queue – I'll wait not anymore!

I sought another place for such as me;
Where I could nurse my bitterness at what I see,
And know some justice, and justification of how I feel,
Assured that Truth was on my side, that Truth was Real!
Yet, should you choose to follow me, I this impart:
Be warned! I found no place in any Heaven for me to rest my weary,
weary heart.
Most certainly there was no harbour that was, for me, a welcoming port.

The Undergraduate Embryologists

By Diana Newson

We took an egg and held it in the light,
to see the softened shadow underswell.
We took a small serrated sterile blade
and sawed a careful hole in the shell.

Sweet square, sweet window in the egg,
We look inside, we see a map of blood.
Dust falls into our embryo,
I add a swirl of sealing wax.

Each day we peer inside. The mass
is growing-coiling-forming out of view.
The work of genes, or God.
We split and spill a few.

The oldest eggs are crammed and full
of soft and slime and claw and thorn.
We scalpel-crack these cradles.
Unready embryos are born.

Observe experimental with dismay,
a monster, tottering and wet.
Note down its horror-shock deformities,
then fetch scissors, for its neck.

The Empty Page
By *Meher Pocha*

Blank paper
burgundy ink
favourite fountain pen
Waiting
Waiting

Come on, all it takes is an hour a day!
Gather together all those memories and visions
vivid characters
perfect storyline
gossamer language
that floated through the sleepless night

Splat! - on the paper
they turn dull and leaden
like squashed dead cockroaches
Quick push away the dust and cobwebs
see if you can capture them
before they drift away

There's lots to do
you didn't get the medal for time-wasting
just like that
but must meals be perfect
must you persevere with German
for the bilingual FaceTime grandchildren
binge read detective stories
binge watch German Krimi
Answer time-gobbling phone calls
Fight hopeless causes

Back to the sloping desk
Determined....
.....Nothing
sentences written and unwritten
with despairing lines struck through

Blank paper
burgundy ink
favourite fountain pen
Waiting
Waiting

Blueberry Pie

By *Stephen Turner*

[For Heather and her family, from Steve, with many happy memories of
1967-69, and my grateful thanks for two years that changed my life, and
also that of my wife, Stephanie, who came with me. For two went out,
and three came back!]

In that harsh winter of 1620,
Cast upon the alien Massachusetts shore,
Persecuted, seeking the love of God, and little more,
I wonder if William Bradford, with friends and family by,
Before spring came, knew sadly that so many of his party would fall ill
and die,
Having, yet – I like to whimsically think - a wish, a vision, *this* hope one
day:
The coming of a hot and tasty blueberry pie!

So that, four hundred years now having passed,
From out the hot belly of the stove, whence I am born,
Plattered to cool, and set aside to stand and rest,
Perhaps already eager eyes upon me, *perhaps* Thanksgiving morn,
Waiting for that anticipated coming of the knife,
That dripping of the juice! that taste! that essence of autumnal life!

And by and by, quite soon I see – I understand it entirely, without
surprise!
Two much-beloved and curly tousled heads appear, two sets of eyes,
Each only just tall enough, to clear the bakehouse board,
Barely able to wait! No patience! With two tongues, the hot blueberry
pie, to be explored!

Incised I am, proportioned I am, in tasty fractions split and formed:

A cold November day, promises of snows to come, four hands that must
　　be warmed.
And in this way - once whole! – I quickly disappear, the platter blank
　　again,
So that, of me, only an overlooked blueberry, and a few crumbs remain.

In years to come, the two tousled heads – still much-beloved – grow tall,
More blueberry pies consumed, sweet potatoes, turkeys, yet – sadly –
　　this is not all,
For foreign fields and foreign circumstances, as they always did, made
　　call,
And in the Fall, upon these foreign fields, a red as red as blueberry juice,
　　for *freedom*, did grossly fall.

The price was paid, for all of us: could not have been foreseen before,
When – blueberry pie or no - William Bradford, and his friends, set
hesitant foot on Plymouth shore.

Iteration

By Erol Hasan

It's happened to you again;
It happens every time.
I feel sympathy for you;
It must be difficult.
You cannot bear to think,
"I am abused; I am mistreated;
They make me suffer;
They diminish me";
So you tell yourself,
"They are good, really;
They cannot help themselves;
They are only doing what was done to them".
That may or not be true;
You perhaps think it heroic,
To love someone in spite of the fact
That they mistreat you;
The more they hurt you, the more so.
And so, the pattern is repeated;
The cycle continues.
Each experience differs in detail from the last;
Time moves forward;
You age.
You learn, but not enough;
So there is change;
Your present ordeal is not the same
As those that preceded it;
But still you suffer.
You may not really want this,
But the defining parameters are your choice;
And a sufficiently wise person could predict how

Your new experience will vary from the one before;
Because you are you,
Your expectations are what they are,
And you give off the same signals;
You chase the same fate.
The fact that you seek it in a different format to the one before,
Does not afford you a better outcome;
Or spare you,
Or those that truly care for you.

Good luck, my friend;
You are back at the beginning;
But the formula of your life is the same,
And always will be;
Unless you find the courage
To consider your past experience,
And see it for what it is.
May God bless you,
For that is beyond my capability.

Renewal?

By Meher Pocha

1985

I walk past the garden
A riot of colour
Red, yellow, magenta, blue
Like paint thrown around
By a wilful child
No quiet pinks and lilacs
For this exuberant gardener

1997

I walk past the garden
A deserted wilderness
The gardener long gone
In a flurry of eulogies
The faithful old dog
Gone to join her
The bitterness of inheritance
Hanging like a thunder cloud
Over the crumbling house

2010

I walk past the garden
Birds and brambles
Rabbit, hedgehog, slow-worm, deer

Red, yellow, blue and white
Wild flowers and old roses
Bringing it back to life
Festoons of ivy
Hiding graffiti on the walls

2018

I walk into the garden
Mine at last!
What shall I do with it?

Biographies

Here are short biographies of some of the contributing authors to this anthology. If an author biography does not appear here, it is because they have chosen not to include it in this anthology.

Paul Green

Paul A. Green's poetry collections include *The Gestaltbunker* (Shearsman Books 2012) and *Shadow Times* (QBS Books 2019) . He has written speculative fiction novels like *The Qliphoth* (Libros Libertad 2007) and *Beneath the Pleasure Zones I and II* (Mandrake 2014, 2016). His radio and stage plays, performed by BBC, CBC, RTE and others, are collected in *Babalon and Other Plays* (Scarlet Imprint 2015). He also writes short stories - one of which won the Fiction Prize at the 2019 Hastings Literary Festival. There's more about his work, including audio and video links, at his website:paulgreenwriter.co.uk.

Diana J. Newson

Diana has a background in science and her career took her to scientific publishing and management, and adult education. After this she trained to be a complementary health practitioner, and is now retired, but caring for her Mum at home. She has always written poetry and one of her first poems was published in the School Magazine (in about 1975, a long time ago!) which was very encouraging. Recently she has been focussing on her poetry and writing more regularly. She has had several poems published in the small press and been highly commended in competitions. Her ambition is to get a pamphlet of poems accepted for publication.

Stephen Turner

Steve is an octogenarian scientist who has written poetry all his life, for his own amusement. He sees his poems as a kind of "photograph" album, reminding him of events, and situations that have gone by. He likes, where possible, to incorporate some social, or scientific, commentary, into his verse. Being "old-fashioned" himself, his poems are also often old-fashioned; they usually rhyme!

Printed in Great Britain
by Amazon